BE ALL YOU CAN BE

Gotham Books

30 N Gould St.
Ste. 20820, Sheridan, WY 82801
https://gothambooksinc.com/

Phone: 1 (307) 464-7800

© 2023 *Michael Ortiz*. All rights reserved.

No part of this book may be reproduced, stored in a retrieval system, or transmitted by any means without the written permission of the author.

Published by Gotham Books (November 14, 2023)

ISBN: 979-8-88775-843-5 (P)
ISBN: 979-8-88775-844-2 (E)

Because of the dynamic nature of the Internet, any web addresses or links contained in this book may have changed since publication and may no longer be valid.

The views expressed in this work are solely those of the author and do not necessarily reflect the views of the publisher, and the publisher hereby disclaims any responsibility for them.

Table of Contents

Dedication v
Foreword vi
Chapter 1: Salina, Kansas 2
Chapter 2: Migrating to Indiana 4
Chapter 3: The Big Surprise 7
Chapter 4: Years 1 and 2 of the Minor Seminary 9
Chapter 5: Years 3 and 4 of the Minor Seminary 12
Chapter 6: Boot Camp 15
Chapter 7: Major Seminary 17
Chapter 9: Ordination and Guadalajara, Mexico 21
Chapter 10: Beyond the Border 23
Chapter 11: First Assignment 25
Chapter 12: The Southern Missions 28
Chapter 13: Volunteering for the Military 30
Chapter 14: Chaplain School & Army Special Forces 32
Chapter 15: Airborne Training 34
Chapter 16: Okinawa. 36
Chapter 17: IV Corps, Vietnam 39
Chapter 18: Special Forces, Vietnam. 41
Chapter 19: A Tour With The 82nd Airborne Division 46
Chapter 20: 10th Special Forces. 47
Chapter 21: Command & General Staff College 50
Chapter 22: Germany and the 1st Infantry Division 51
Chapter 23: From Fort Benning to Carlisle Barracks 52
Chapter 24: Panama 53
Chapter 25: From Texas to Colorado 56
Chapter 26: Arlington 58
Chapter 27: Civilian Assignments 60
Chapter 28: Retirement. 62
Acknowledgments 65

Dedication

I dedicate this booklet to my parents whose love for God, Country and Family inspired me to be

All that I wanted to be.

Foreword

Sometimes our insights come to us in strange and unexpected ways. Not long ago, while channel surfing through TV land, I caught part of the Larry King Live program. The host was interviewing a varied group of celebrities, including most successful basketball coach Mike Krzyzewski, Rachel Scdoris (a legally blind woman who competed in the Iditarod world famous dog sled race), and Ron Howard (a former child star turned world famous film director). An auditorium packed with college students listened intently as Larry asked each individual for the secret to their success.

I was struck by the similarity of responses from this diverse group of people. All acknowledged there had been a certain person in their lives whom they admired and tried to imitate, but they had each also come to realize that much more was required of them than simply looking up to and imitating this role model. Each celebrity told Larry, in different words, that a burning desire to excel in their chosen field was essential to their success. They spoke of a passion to be the best, a passion that demanded constant hours of training, dedication, and sacrifice to achieve their goal. To this, Mike Krzyzewski added, "When I stop having the passion, I should leave." This drive to succeed is not unique to these individuals—I have read about other exemplary athletes in sports magazines who share a similar outlook. Eric Weihenmayer, for example, was legally blind, yet he became the first and only blind man to climb to the summit of Mount Everest. LaDanien Tomlinson (the Charger's outstanding running back). When he and his wife lost their "first=born" he told one of San Diego's staff writers: "I look at things in a different light. For one, nobody is invincible. Everybody goes through difficult situations in their life. The key is to handle those situations. You can blame others or you can look at things in a positive way and overcome them and be a different person."

The origin of this book stems from an interaction with a noncelebrity a young soldier working as an Honor Guard at Arlington National Cemetery. It was this young man who convinced me that other people would be interested in reading about my experiences as a priest and Army Chaplain. They would want to know, he said, what made me do what I did and choose what I chose in my life. This account of my life, then, is an attempt to provide answers to that young soldier and anyone else drawn to understand what motivates a person to achieve things in life. Just like Larry King's interviewees, I hope that my own experiences show that doing things with a passion can have positive and surprising results.

Remembering back to my earliest days, I can see now that I unconsciously did some things in my life with a passion even as a child. one of my aunts often liked to tell me that I was a proud and stubborn child. Even though those observations hurt me at the time, I recognized that it was not pride that made me choose options that others my age did not even consider—it was a determination to excel and make something of myself, no matter what that would take.

BE ALL YOU CAN BE

Fr. Mike Ortiz

Chapter 1:
Salina, Kansas

I was born in Salina Kansas (the very center of the continental United States, as my first-grade teacher would often remind us). My parents had emigrated from Mexico with their parents in search of a better life, and it was in Salina that my parents met, fell in love, and married.

My father worked for the railroad, while my mother got a job plucking chickens in a local processing company. In addition to being my birth year, 1929 was also the beginning of the Great Depression, and I believe that my roots at that time of political struggle inspired my desire to take nothing for granted.

I recall little about my early childhood, except an awareness of the sacrifices my parents had to make in order to make ends meet. As poor as we were, my mother somehow managed to have her children cleanly dressed, even though our clothes might have come from the rummage sale at our parish hall. Looking back now, I marvel at my parents' strength and persistence during those very difficult times.

Because of my father's job on the railroad, we moved frequently from one small Kansas town to another. I can even recall living in a converted railroad "Boxcar" provided by the Acheson Topeka & Santa Fe railroad Company. It was divided into two bedrooms and a kitchen. The ribbed coal stove in the center served as heater and kitchen stove, the water came from a small water pump just outside, and there was an "outhouse" a few hundred yards away from our home.

The first priority for my mother after each move was to enroll me in a local catholic school, (if there was one in the town) a goal she somehow managed to attain despite our poverty. I was determined to do well in school in appreciation of her efforts. She obviously placed great value on a Catholic school education, a value that even as a youngster I came to share.

When I was old enough to understand, my father talked to me about the discrimination that was common at that time, such as the "NO GREASERS ALLOWED" signs posted on restaurant bathroom entrances. I personally do not recall experiencing this kind of discrimination, and I really didn't understand what he was trying to tell me at the time. I do, however, remember often thinking that someday I would do something special. I didn't know what that something special would be, but I was determined that I would be different, that I would stand out, and that I would achieve the goals I set for myself. Was this the pride in me? Perhaps.

Despite these lofty ambitions, I got into my fair share of mischief, as young kids from poor neighborhoods often do. I grew up with an uncle who was a few years older than me, and we became close companions as well as "partners in crime." We bragged about what we were going to be when we grew up—soldiers like one of our uncles, or priests like those in our parish (they were the only adults we saw often). Like kids everywhere, we also wanted to act "grown up" and to try adult things. I recall, for example, getting the sticks used for holding up balloons, lighting them, and inhaling them like cigarettes. When that didn't bring enough satisfaction, we learned to take the tobacco from the cigarette butts we salvaged, roll them up in newspaper, and smoke them where we thought we would not get caught. Alcohol was another beckoning adventure, leading me to sneak into my grandfather's tool shed to sample the beer he had just brewed in a large tub. On the more positive side, I have a clear memory of my uncle playing priest and making me his "altar server", a role he saw befitting based on my status as the younger one and a young girl as the parishioner. I kind of enjoyed this.

Chapter 2:
Migrating to Indiana

While in Salina, my mother gave birth to two brothers and a sister resulting in circumstances that prompted our move to another state. It was some time after I completed the third or fourth grade that my father moved all of us to Indiana. A brother-in-law had advised him that the steel mills in East Chicago Indiana provided better pay than the railroad company in Salina, Kansas. With four children to feed and clothe, the move to Indiana to pursue better economic opportunities was the right decision, although it did not seem so at the time. It took weeks before my father was hired, so we were forced to apply for the government relief program. We were also living with an uncle and his family of four, making for tight quarters until my father could find an apartment for our family. He eventually found us an apartment in the center of the city about a mile and a half from his new job, close enough for him to walk to work to. We definitely couldn't afford an automobile so we all walked even to the school we attended. There were several public schools in the area, and the church we attended was only a half block away, so we were all pleased when we settled into our new home in the city.

I was the oldest of what became a family of fourteen children. My mother obviously had her hands full, so she tasked me with the grocery shopping. I remember heading off to the store, no matter the weather, with her carefully penciled grocery list and the government relief coupons that helped keep food on the table. It was not only the government that reached out with a helping hand in those difficult times. The priests at the church were also aware of our need and called my mother before church rummage sales to allow her to pick out whatever clothing our family needed before the opening the church basement on the following day.

After our move to Indiana, my mother initially enrolled me in public school. She just couldn't afford the tuition required for attending a catholic school.

Young as I was, I felt a definite difference between the public school and the Catholic school I had attended in Kansas. Once again, my mother did all in her power to get me into the local Catholic school, and we paid the tuition in whatever installments we could afford. The sisters who taught at the school helped us with gifts of surplus food and donated clothing—acts of kindness that made an impression on me. Although my relatives had once accused me of being proud, necessity overcame pride even when I was teased by classmates because of a worn shirt or pair of worn trousers. Whatever embarrassment this might have caused at the time, I realized that the clothes I wore to school were always clean and ironed. My pride in my mother's high standards and ability to make the best of things far surpassed the discomfort caused by my classmates' unkind words. In my formative grade-school years, I began to develop special interests. Spelling, history, and art were my favorite subjects, and football and boxing were my favorite sports. I also became interested in the military. Whenever a rep from a Military Academy visited my eighth-grade, I would be the one most interested. I prayed that my parents could find a way to pay for my attending the military Academy. I wanted to show people that my family might be poor, but we could do anything that anyone else could do. I guess I was out to prove to the world that this Mexican kid from Kansas could do anything he set his mind to. Because we lived so close to our parish church, it was natural that I went there and met other young people my age. My mother eventually suggested that I volunteer to be an altar server. (Good old Mom).

My father had already volunteered to help the priests with whatever work was needed, and I began assisting at funerals, and wedding Masses. Many were the mornings my mother roused me from my bed and sent me over to serve the morning Mass. Her passion and determination undoubtedly had a great impact on my development of those religious traits.

Helping out became part of the fabric of my life both at home and in the church. I found I enjoyed helping others. I was also drawn deeper into parish life by the energy of the young associate priests who worked with the youth. Our parish, poor though it may have been, soon became the most popular in a city of at least four catholic churches. I joined the CYO (Catholic Youth Organization) in our parish and participated in the many programs it offered. I enjoyed this part of my young life, which planted and nourished the seeds of my vocation. Through my altar service, close association with the parish priests, and involvement in the youth programs, I began thinking about becoming a priest and telling myself that serving as a priest might not be such a bad idea. I didn't dare say anything about these thoughts to anyone else though because the future seemed so far away.

As our family grew in size, my father took on extra jobs in addition to his regular work at the steel mill to make ends meet. I felt that, as the oldest child, I too should be helping, so I got my first job as a paper boy and proudly turned over the few dollars I made to my mother. During the seventh grade, I got a job as a stock boy in one of the city's clothing stores. Again, the check I received went to my mother, who gave me enough change to pay for a movie on Sundays. All of this was done without question, in obedience and love. This was simply the way it was.

As one grade of school gave way to another, I began thinking more seriously about my future. What high school would I be attending? Did I intend to prepare for college? What about the idea of volunteering for the military?

Young as I was during the summer vacations, I often gathered a few of my brothers and friends and organized them into military units (I falsely imagined I knew enough about the military). I was able to "scrounge" some old army uniforms and equipment, and we would hike to the outskirts of town to play our war games. Our weapons were the standard Red Ryder BB guns that young boys loved. Most of my classmates talked about the Marines when we talked about joining the military, and I thought about that too, but then there was the priesthood. Was that the way I should go? Gradually these thoughts about the future were set aside in order to deal with more immediate realities. The future would have to wait. For the present, I planned to attend the popular public school in town, the school where almost everyone went, and the school with the best basketball and football team in the state.

Chapter 3:
The Big Surprise

Right after my graduation from eighth grade, I enrolled in the public school and immediately signed up for the football team. Playing football meant I could not get a job because of the intense training during the summer, but it also meant that I finally had a chance to be something special to help my dad. At this time, I was also thinking that I might get into the military, in fact, a cousin of mine and I had attempted to sign up at a local post office, but we were turned away because of our age. "HA"! The time wasn't yet right for the military. Instead, I spent the summer months drilling on the high school football field, and practicing as hard as I could to make the junior varsity team. It was an exciting and challenging time for me. This was big time!

As summer came to an end, the high school coach picked me for the varsity football team and I was all set to play my first real football game. I was throwing my whole heart into it, giving it my all. One day during a scrimmage, the coach called me to the bench where I saw one of the priests from my parish. I wondered if something happened at home? Or perhaps, I had I done something wrong? I waited for the worst. When Father Will, our associate pastor, told me he just wanted to talk to me, I wondered what in the world this was all about, little suspecting that my whole future was about to change dramatically.

Nothing could have prepared me for Father's question: "Have you given any thought to becoming a priest?" I turned red in the face and broke out in a sweat. "Where did you get that idea, Father?" I blurted out, "I've never said a word to anyone about this." His response surprised me almost as much as his question. "Well, son," he said, "there are things about a person that friends and teachers see without being mentioned. Your eighth-grade teacher called us and asked whether one of the parish priests could talk to you because she felt that you might have a calling to the priesthood." He paused before adding, "If you think you might want to study for the priesthood, now is the time to make your decision, not four years from now. It takes twelve years of long and difficult study before a man is ordained."

I was truly shocked to the core of my being by all of this, especially the need to make an immediate decision. Talk about being hit by a ton of bricks! Father had grabbed my attention, and then proceeded to exhibit excellent recruiting skills as he made everything sound so challenging. The seminary, he said, was just like a small version of the UNIVERSITY OF NOTRE DAME. "Really?", I loved that idea because I imagined life in the minor seminary was probably just like being on a large college campus (regretfully though, it would not be a co-educational life). I envisioned large classrooms, a gymnasium, swimming pool, and athletic fields and a lot of girls. The required twelve years of hard study did not in truth appeal much to me, except for the fact that I would receive an education that my parents would never be able to afford.

I told Father that I would think about it and discuss my decision with my parents. "Fine," he smiled, "I'll give you a week to decide. You will have to drop out of this school, get your parents to pack your bag, and I will personally drive you and your parents to the seminary this coming Sunday. But you must hurry." He assumed that the whole decision was a done deal! I know now that he was sure I was going to accept the challenge. The unstated, and as yet unlived theme of my life—challenge the ordinary and become extraordinary—was beginning to take shape and become reality.

There is no doubt that I shocked my parents and some of our relatives when I told them what I wanted to do. "Go to the seminary?" they asked in astonished amazement. Didn't I realize that as the oldest son I should instead prepare to help support my family? My parents quickly understood my desire and approved of my decision to pursue the goal of priesthood. However, there were a few aunts and uncles who flat out told me that I would never make it, that I was too worldly and too interested in girls. Their arguments became a challenge to me and I thought to myself, I'll show you! I excitedly accompanied my Dad to a Jewish section in Chicago called Maxwell Street with dozens of outdoor clothing booths which sold almost any type of clothing one might need in attending a "collage" and definitely affordable for a poor family sending their son away to college.

Chapter 4:
Years 1 and 2 of the Minor Seminary

It was a beautiful, sunny September afternoon when I bid farewell to my brothers, sisters, and relatives. My mother, father, and I piled into our priest's automobile and drove east on Highway 30 to Donaldson Indiana I would be living about 80 miles from home, and my parents had promised that they would come every month on Visitors' Sunday. Anticipation and excitement filled me as we drove from city to country, but my excitement quickly turned to fear when I saw the marker that read "Donaldson "Unincorporated"! I stared out the window and saw only one small general store, a gas station, and a post office. Other than these buildings, all we could see were rows and rows of corn, we were completely surrounded by cornfields. The only traffic light in town was for the railroad crossing, which led to a long asphalt road that stretched out into farmland. We drove for about a mile on this road, passing barns, cornfields, and a few farmhouses. My fear escalated to near panic as we crossed the railroad tracks, and Father suddenly turned left onto another narrow asphalt road. This road cut through the cornfields, and led to a solitary three story brick building, which strongly resembled a cigar box. That's it? One lonely three-story red brick building? As I looked past the building, I saw a number of kids running around in a briar patch. They seemed to be playing touch football and in their street clothes—no yard markers, no uniforms. Where were the manicured lawns, the tall shade trees? The place was desolate, and all I could see were just rows and rows of corn! My dreams of life on a beautiful college campus crumbled into dust.

I turned around to look at my parents and good "sweet-talking Padre" to tell them I wasn't staying, but all of a sudden, the students and faculty teachers (all priests) stopped their game and ran over to welcome us, (especially me). I was the new Mexican-American kid that the faculty had been telling them about. It was such a warm welcome by kids who perhaps had never even known someone of Mexican descent, and I felt that they would challenge me in a good way. I thought, "All right, Lord, if this is a challenge, I accept it." I was still tempted to get back in the car and go back home but I was also stubborn enough to bid goodbye to Father and my parents. Someday, I would very likely thank Father.

Over the years I have often looked back on that moment in time, and I believe the only thing that kept me there that Sunday was the large number of boys my age enjoying themselves—despite their surprising surroundings! They had arrived several weeks earlier and had gotten to know each other even though they came from all over the country. It was their warm welcome to my parents and me that changed my mood and drew me into the friendship they were offering. I thought to myself, "If they can take this, then I certainly can at least try it." That apparently inborn toughness and determination in the face of unexpected, unpleasant circumstances was my saving grace once again. I was certainly not the only one with adjustment difficulties. It was not unusual to hear sniffles coming from some of the bunk beds after lights out in the dormitory, and sometimes I would learn a few days later that the homesickness that had prompted the sniffles had led to a departure from the seminary. I was determined to never leave for that reason alone. I put up with the full days of study, the institutional type meals, the flag football games on the briar patch fields, and the other required sacrifices. I also worked like a horse to get through the four years of minor seminary. Many of our professors had escaped being drafted into the "Hitler Youth" in Nazi Germany. Needless to say, they were strict, "no nonsense type teachers.

On the brighter side, some of us lived close enough to Donaldson that we had relatives coming to see us once a month on the much-anticipated Visiting Sunday. We were also allowed to write home once a month, which I suppose helped us slowly break our close ties to the familiar. At Christmas, we were given a two-week vacation, permitting us all to spend some precious time with our families during the holidays. And then there were summer vacations, a space of time we all eagerly looked forward to. A memorable highlight of this difficult seminary period occurred when the superior obtained tickets for us to attend a Notre Dame football game (a "real" College football game). Now this was the real campus I had dreamed about! The many buildings, athletic department, and huge football stadium were in stark contrast to the institution in which I was enrolled.

Returning home that first year for summer vacation, I found my brothers and sisters to be far more grown up than when I had last seen them. Some of my uncles had gone off to fight in World War II, in both Europe and the Pacific. I felt a certain envy of them, but I still was not old enough to enlist. I decided instead to help the war effort and earn enough money to pay my tuition at the seminary. Evidently the war effort was able to use my help because, although I was underage, I got a job working for the New York Central, which passed through our city. I had no idea how hard my father had worked until I myself worked on a railroad gang. I learned very quickly to respect the many laborers with whom I worked. My mother always took my paycheck and reminded me that it was going toward my tuition. I was happy to be able to contribute and to feel that I was no longer a burden to my overburdened parents. At this point, I had nine brothers and sisters.

Summer came and went all too quickly. Before I realized it, I was back in the other world of the seminary. There were fewer classmates this year, but we were now sophomores and more accepted by upper classmen. One of the first things I noticed as I reunited with my fellow seminarians was that I had matured more than most of them, both physically and mentally. I attributed this to the fact that I had done hard labor alongside grown men and had also come to understand the value of the dollar.

The academic subjects seemed somewhat easier, probably because our freshman year had taught us how to study and apply ourselves. I continued to struggle with some subjects though, and I still secretly envied those who didn't seem to have to study long hours to master the material. Ironically, these were some of the very classmates who left the seminary, while those of us who were challenged by our studies continued to struggle and stay the course.

Chapter 5:
Years 3 and 4 of the Minor Seminary

After my sophomore year, I got a summer job working in the very steel mill in which my father and some of my uncles worked. I was underage, but because many of our men were fighting in World War II, the mills needed "man power" and so, I was quickly hired. They did require that I wear a badge stating I was underage, however, a requirement that greatly displeased me. From my perspective, if I was man enough to keep up with the older men, then I should be man enough to not have to wear a discriminating badge!

I had thought working on the railroad was tough. Well, let me tell you that making steel, curing it, cutting it, and shipping it far surpassed the effort and energy required while working on tracks and ties. The special steel plates are the very flooring plates manufactured for our Navy's submarines so ...I felt patriotic. I worked three different shifts at the steel mill, changing the routine every week. At day's end I was so tired I had no desire to socialize or go out with friends. In fact, I looked forward to summer being over so that I could return to the seminary! I gladly turned over my paycheck to my mother because I knew that this might be my last opportunity to help with the family finances. The job at the steel mill paid well, and I knew I was making a substantial contribution that summer.

The last two years in the minor seminary at Donaldson were just as tough as the first two, although my physical and mental maturity had changed me considerably. I felt surer of myself and was more willing to make sacrifices to reach whatever goal I chose. Life was educating and toughening me. I learned from those around me—the upperclassmen, the workers on the railroad and in the steel mills, and my parents. I heard clearcut messages from the lives of these role models: "Reach out for a worthwhile goal!" "Don't be a "quitter" when the going gets tough!" "Make the sacrifice!" "Do it with a passion!", "BE ALL YOU CAN BE!"

It was around this time that many of us also began to realize that there were other humans besides boys in the world. Girls started to notice us and we began to notice them. Even while at the seminary, some managed to find a way to start up a conversation with some of the local teenagers. I myself met one of the most beautiful girls I have ever seen during summer vacation my in junior year. I had quit my job several weeks before returning to the seminary that year, and my mother suggested I take a vacation to New York City and visit an aunt who was a Catholic nun assigned there. I took my first train ride to the "BIG APPLE" and surprised my aunt. She of course lived in a convent, so she arranged for me to live in the local Catholic Rectory where a few Franciscan Monks welcomed me. They even volunteered to accompany me to Brooklyn where one of my classmates, (Peter) lived. It was memorable.

Exiting the subway in the Flatbush area of Brooklyn, we walked a few blocks to Pete's family's two-story apartment building. We rang the doorbell to the apartment, and the most beautiful young girl opened the door and immediately yelled out my name. "LUPE (my baptismal nickname?" "Yes, that's me," I said, "but how on earth do you know my name?" She replied, "Oh, Peter has been talking about you so much, I just know you are the one." I immediately felt right at home as I met Pete's mother and his four sisters. But that beautiful Irish sister of my friend caught my eye and heart. We got along just fine. I spent a few short days enjoying the company of this wonderful family, but especially the personal tour of New York with my classmate and his beautiful sister, Kathleen. I must confess, I had a tough decision to make. I just couldn't get Pete's sister out of my decision making, but we were both teenagers in high school, and we lived miles apart.

I realized I first needed to get a college education after the minor seminary, and then decide whether to continue my studies for the priesthood or pick another profession that would allow me to pursue that one young girl to whom I was so attracted. I found out years later that this girl had also felt an attraction, but because she believed I was totally committed to finishing my studies and entering the priesthood, she gave up hope, met a young man, married him, and had five wonderful children. This became one more of the unseen sacrifices I felt I had to make on the way to my goal, a sacrifice with unknown impact on another person as well as on myself. If not for the fact that we were both only in high school, separated by distance, and I still had years of study, my life might have turned out very differently. Our friendship has lasted to this day, however, and I believe the pull to pursue my two dreams (priesthood and military service) was the strongest.

Our senior year at the seminary was a busy one. We learned the material that regular high school students were being taught, and we could at least read Latin, German, and Greek. This knowledge was very useful because some of the courses we were to take in the major seminary, such as philosophy and theology, were taught in Latin. At the conclusion of senior year, we were not allowed to go home for summer vacation. Instead, we spent our time doing chores, preparing the place for the next group of incoming freshmen, and taking classes on Spirituality. Then we moved on to our next destination, the "Novitiate", located in southern Illinois.

Chapter 6:
Boot Camp

On a sunny June afternoon in 1947 the class of '47, which had been whittled down to just twelve out of the original thirty-four, were driven to a little town called Ste Marie Illinois. Upon our arrival, we were greeted by a lone bespeckled, slight man in a black cassock, and were assigned to what would be our "Cell" for the next year. It truly was a cell— a partitioned by ten-foot half walls with a white sheet covering the entrance, a small washbasin with a small pitcher of water and one hard straw-mattress cot. The corded whip hanging on the wall scared the daylights out of me. What had I signed up for this time?

After hanging the few bits of clothing, we had brought, we were guided to a classroom, the place where we would spend most of our time. We received a Bible and a copy of a *Spiritual book we called "RODRIGUEZ"* (a kind of tour guide to the spiritual life). Our briefing consisted of a seemingly oppressive list of do's and don'ts. All smoking material was to be turned in. Any money in our possession was also to be turned in, as were radios, magazines, mundane reading material—in short: "everything" was to be turned in! Hardly anything mundane was allowed. Can you imagine how difficult it was for the smokers to give up smoking, or the radio "afficionados" to give up their pocket radios? One classmate who had nicotine-stained fingers would suck on his fingers until the stained fingers disappeared. Silence was to be observed almost all the time. And…. remember the whip I had seen hanging on my cell wall? Well, that was for the "little discipline" we were to inflict on ourselves every Friday evening before going to bed. From this moment on, our mail was to be censored, and we could not read any newspapers or listen to the radio under any circumstances. I was stunned by the sudden discipline being imposed on us, and it was to be enforced by a timid-looking priest who had greeted us upon our arrival! This is when I began secretly calling our Novice Master "The Sarge."

In September we began our official year of developing spiritually and learning the rules and regulations of the religious order that we were striving to enter, the Priests of the Sacred Heart. We began wearing our "uniforms" (black cassocks). The parallels between the novitiate and the military were uncanny, A reader who has ever gone through basic training in the military will perhaps understand the kind of situation in which I found myself. Here, after more than my years at the minor seminary, I was tempted to just quit and leave. In fact, the novice master once called me while I was throwing around a football to suggest that I drop out of the class. I was "too worldly" he claimed. That suggestion was to me a challenge, a dare, and I was bold enough to tell him that I had no intention of quitting, and that I would do my best to comply with whatever was demanded of me. That little bespeckled priest (Novice Master) had challenged me and I would die before giving up. This year of trial would either make or break me. I maintained my sanity by keeping physically active, participating in any sport I could conjure up, and volunteering to cut lawns and work on the farm, all the while fighting hard to learn some humility. If steel were iron tested in the furnace, then this year of novitiate definitely qualified as a "white hot furnace" of near biblical proportions. In later years I underwent quite a bit of training in the military, but I still consider the novitiate as a landmark, a trying and tough period of mental and spiritual testing.

Upon completion of the year as Novices, ten of us graduated (were 'professed', as it was officially called), meaning we took the vows of poverty, chastity, and obedience in accordance with the requirements of the Priests of the Sacred Heart. Our relatives were invited to the ceremony, and my proud parents, along with a few uncles and aunts, drove down from Indiana. Pete's family drove all the way from Brooklyn, and again I met my friend Kathleen (with a boyfriend) and her mother and sisters. All went well, and I prepared for the next step—attending a real college.

Although the seven years left before ordination seemed like a lifetime, there was still an overwhelming sensation of emotional relief, and I felt like I could breathe again. I felt that I had made the right decision and had accomplished what I was striving to achieve. I was truly proud of having stuck it out and was anxious to get the education I felt I needed. I was also happy that my parents didn't have to worry about tuition. The religious order to which I belonged would fund my studies in philosophy and theology because I had taken the vows of poverty, chastity and obedience. At the same time, I wasn't completely sure about my future because I still had a burning desire to somehow find a way to join the military.

Chapter 7:
Major Seminary

In early September—so long a time of transition in my life—we were driven up to what would be our new home for eight years. The drive was a beautiful one, and since parents and relatives had been allowed to accompany us, there was a sense of freedom that pervaded the group. Freedom is never so sweet as when experienced after captivity. We could now smoke if we wanted to, read the papers, listen to the radio, and talk all we wanted.

Things were certainly looking up, especially given the Monastery location among the rolling green hills of Wisconsin. The Foto to the left is one we lived in years ago; The new monastery building is a modern "Theologate "and now Offers preparatory classes for many Diocesan students. It is surrounded by plenty of pine trees, a number of athletic fields as well as a small lake. What a difference from Donaldson or the novitiate!

After meeting the upperclassmen and faculty, we felt a bit more mature physically and mentally, and had a desire to grow spiritually. The changes that took place were difficult at times, and even here I lost a few of my classmates. I was tempted, but I was stubborn enough to hang in and fight the temptation to quit. I needed the education. Starting my freshman year of college (I felt so proud now) meant that I had accomplished what no one in my family had yet accomplished. My parents and most of my relatives were proud of me, although one of my aunts commented, "You'll never make it. You are too worldly!" I whispered under my breath, "I'll show you, you old Bitty!" Some of my studies were tough but others were interesting and pleasantly challenging. I continued to believe that no matter the academic struggles all would be beneficial to me no matter the path I would choose to take.

As in the minor seminary, most of our professors were from Germany. Many were forced into Hitler's military service, but had eventually escaped and became priests, and religious brothers. But I found myself still thinking about the military.

During my years in this major seminary, I learned to be the barber for both students and faculty, so this was my chief job during our daily work periods. Since I had always loved art, I also became the artist for the seminary magazine, and eventually its editor. I mention these extracurricular activities because that was how I challenged myself and brought balance to the mental tasks that faced me as a student. I may not have been the smartest in my class, but I once again felt the need to prove to others that I was good at something!

There was also another theme I perceived in these years. As during our earlier educational periods, I noticed that it was the academically gifted students who were most likely to quit or drop out of studies. These were the students who never had to "cram" for exams, and who could recall what they learned in class by reading it just once. It occurred to me that perhaps things that came too easily were not too highly valued. I, on the other hand, had to burn the midnight oil often, but I stuck to it. I was still hanging in, perhaps subtly motivated not only by my desire to prove myself, but also by my belief that persistence itself was of great value.

By the time we finished our philosophy studies, there were only about six of us left out of the original thirty-four. Our Provincial Superior (the US "superior"), decided to give us a break from our studies by sending two of us to study at the International Seminary in Rome "The Eternal City," and another one to work at St. Joseph Indian School and one to work on a newly acquired 250-acre farm in Northeastern Pennsylvania. (Honesdale). Guess who got the farm? I, the city boy from the outskirts of Chicago, spent a year farming. Little did I dream that this was all to prepare me for the future. I did not object, but rather took this move as another challenge. I wanted to learn everything I could about farming and do it well. Achieving this goal meant getting up before daylight, bringing in the cows for milking, cleaning the barn, shoveling manure, mowing fields to make hay, bailing the hay, and snow plowing in the winter . . . talk about learning new skills! This kind of learning was a welcome change from classes and books. The hard work helped me to develop physically (and mature). recreation consisted of walking through the woods on the property, watching the deer jump over our fences from the adjacent game preserve, killing the ground hogs who damaged our fields, and, of course, hunting deer and turkey. This was a whole new world for me, and I had a ball! In fact, I guess they liked my work enough because my Fr. Provincial requested that I return to the farm during the next summer break, after completion of another year of studies in Wisconsin.

With philosophy behind us, entering theology was one step closer to the priesthood. As a result, our studies were geared more toward what a priest would need for his ministry. With this increased emersion in priestly studies, I realized clearly that the time was approaching for me to make up my mind regarding my vocation. I thought of the special girl I had not been in contact with for years, of the military life that I was attracted to, and of the thirteen brothers and sisters that my father still worked so hard to provide for. At the same time, I noticed how my father beamed with pride as he talked about his son who was going to be a priest. I found out that he was even putting aside some money in preparation for my Ordination gift. When I showed him a sketch of the chalice, I dreamed of one day possessing. he told me to have it made as I wished and that this would be my family's ordination gift.

In the last year before ordination, I received the order of "Sub-Diaconate" which was followed a few months later by the "Diaconate", the final step to the goal I had set for myself. Six months before I was to be ordained, a life-shattering event occurred. My father was rushed to the hospital and was diagnosed with an "aneurism". The oldest of my sisters made an urgent call to me suggesting I leave immediately to Dad's hospital bed in Indiana. Given the news, I immediately told the superior (who, ironically, was the very "drill instructor" who thought I was not fit for the priesthood back in my Novitiate days) that I was going home on emergency leave. He advised me to be patient and wait until I received more information regarding my father's condition. I fought for control of myself in the face of this advice, until just a few hours later when my sister called to break the news that our father had passed away. I became so angry that I blurted out some emotionally explosive words and told the superior that I was leaving for the funeral whether he gave permission or not. I knew enough about the vow of obedience I had taken to realize that I was putting my future on the line, but at the moment it did not matter to me.

On the way home, during the preparations for the funeral, and at the burial, my thoughts focused on my mother and all of my brothers and sisters, and what the future held for them. One brother serving in the Navy had flown back from Japan where he was stationed, but not on time for the Funeral Service. Another brother who was a year younger than I had already served his tour of duty in Korea and had gotten a job at the Steel Mill. The rest of my siblings were still young and in school. Being the oldest, I felt that I had to make what was perhaps the biggest decision I would ever have to make—remain in the seminary and be ordained in six months, or come home to take care of my mother, brothers, and sisters. My father had so looked forward to seeing me ordained. My mother courageously assured me that she could manage the family while my next younger brother, had gotten a job in the steel mill, and would provide the greatly needed financial support. In addition, my brother serving in the Navy would soon be discharged and promised to help support the family. I was torn, feeling the immense responsibility of caring for my family, while at the same time knowing how much my family, especially my father, wanted me to become a priest. Finally, with the realization that my family would be cared for, I knew that I had an obligation to continue to pursue my dream of becoming a priest, and to do so with a passion! "BE ALL YOU CAN BE"!

Chapter 9:
Ordination and Guadalajara, Mexico

On May 26, 1956, my dream became reality. I was ordained at the cathedral in Milwaukee, Wisconsin and couldn't have been happier, and sadder. I could almost see the smile and pride on my dad's face, looking sixty-four, I had stayed the course and achieved this goal. Ordination Day was one of the happiest days of my life, marred only by the absence of my father. My brothers and sisters, uncles and aunts, and mother had driven up from Indiana to witness a beautiful and moving day. They had someone in the family who was now a priest and were very happy I had made it. Some called it a miracle.

A week later I celebrated my first mass at my hometown parish in Indiana. The church was not large enough to accommodate all who wanted to attend, so it was decided that the Solemn Mass would be celebrated in the church parking lot! I was the first priest the parish had produced, so the priests, nuns, and parishioners went all out to make this a memorable occasion. Many of my peers, classmates from grade school, friends from youth organizations, and "old-timers" who knew me as a kid came together to celebrate, making this day truly significant and a lifelong memory. I still had to return to the seminary in September to complete my studies. The time spent in my home parish brought with the realization that I knew very little Spanish despite having a Spanish surname. I felt obliged to do something about that situation, which motivated me to be brash enough to approach my regional superior and ask for permission to find a seminary that included Spanish as a second language and would accept me and allow me to complete my last year of studies there while simultaneously learning Spanish. The only major seminary he found was in Mexico and he would make all arrangements and…I could go.

I was thrilled, not only because I would be traveling outside my country for the first time, but also because I was leaving the place, I had lived in for the last seven years. Into these carefully laid plans, however, came an unexpected problem—a technical difficulty that almost prevented me from going to Mexico. When I applied for a student visa, the Mexican consulate failed to inform me that the Mexican government did not approve seminaries as places of study. Thus, when I flew into Mexico City, I was refused entry, and both my passport and visa were withheld until I returned to the United States. I was furious and determined to return, having no intention of allowing my dream to be thwarted by a technicality. Following the advice of an apologetic Consular in Chicago, I returned to Mexico through a different route, and this time I brought a tourist visa and dressed like a "Gringo Tourist" Upon arriving, I made contact with the American Council. He had a good laugh and took me to "Chapalita" (a suburb of Guadalajara) for a delicious Mexican dinner and a Marriachi for entertainment. After this trying ordeal, I came away with the impression that I had outsmarted the system that had so capriciously tried to block this important goal of mine.

Chapter 10:
Beyond the Border

I must confess that I experienced a kind of culture shock upon my arrival in Mexico. I may have been of Mexican descent, but that was all the background I had. I knew little Spanish, and I also knew nothing about my heritage or the customs of this new country in which I was to live. On the opening day of classes, it seemed like the entire student body of the seminary, as well as the faculty, were curious about the newly ordained priest from the US. Everyone wanted to try out their English on me, and I struggled to understand what they were saying. The rector of the seminary was extremely understanding and helpful, giving me special treatment that bordered on the preferential.

Initially, I could not understand whether the professors were teaching in Spanish or Latin because of the accent. (And partial ignorance of both languages). Fortunately, I gradually became able to decipher what was being taught. Once the students and faculty understood that I was determined to learn Spanish, they became very helpful and even challenging. One of my instructors, a distinguished looking Monsignor, who happened to be one of the professors in their seminary helped me immensely in my efforts to learn Spanish. He asked the Rector of this Major Seminary to allow me to celebrate Masses in his parish on Sundays as well as weekdays. This began as an easy assignment because at that time everything was still said in Latin. I purchased a Bike and rode to the inner city for Mass. Then, after several weeks of this comfortable routine, the pastor asked me to give the Sunday homily in my Mass, in Spanish. I was scared to death! I told the kind Monsignor I would have to first write my sermon in English and then translate and read it in Spanish. How wise that priest turned out to be. By preparing the Sunday homily, first in English and then translated into Spanish I was forced to really concentrate and quickly learn whatever vocabulary I needed to convey my thoughts to the people.

During a "break "my professor friends invited me to participate in a tour of Mexico's dormant volcano and climb to the very top. Was this a challenge for their "Gringo Padre"? I accepted it as a dare. I would show them. Upon our arrival our small group camped at the base of "EL VOLCAN" overnight. Sometime during the night, I became terribly ill with diarrhea and heavy sweating. One of the priests recommended that I remain behind at the campsite while they continued the climb up the volcano. I thought perhaps they felt that their friend from America couldn't take it, though that was certainly not expressed. But I did notice a kind of "DARE" Taking that perceived thought as my motivation, I told them that I would continue the climb with them. This became for me a case of mind over matter, a "do or die" situation, yet another challenge I was determined to meet.

One of my professor buddies had brought along a flask of mescal, (a potent drink like tequila). Mixing it with some snow, in a small paper cup. I gulped down the potent brew. My whole insides began to burn, but the drink provided me the strength to reach the very top of the volcano where I proudly signed my name to the book chained to a metal box. I felt proud as the priests congratulated me for "hanging in" there and not giving up"

Chapter 11:
First Assignment

The ten months in Mexico went by all too quickly. After our oral exams in Latin and Spanish (a now familiar language), one of my sisters and two of my brothers drove down from Indiana to bring me back to the US. Of course, it was a good excuse for them to have their big brother as their tour guide, and now a bit more knowledgeable in Spanish. They simply loved Guadalajara, Mexico City, the pyramids, our parents' birthplace, but most of all the comradery of clergy and seminarians. Upon my return to "the States", I spent a few days with the rest of our family, and then they brought me back to Hales Corners to get my first assignment.

Since I had asked for the opportunity to learn Spanish, I thought it was logical that my assignment would be in a bilingual parish. It was payback time, or so I thought. To my surprise, I was told that I was assigned as associate pastor to my home parish, the very place where I had made my decision to go to the seminary some twelve years earlier. I knew many of the parishioners, especially the young people with whom I grew up, so in a very real sense it was like coming home.

The pastor, a large, intelligent, priest, originally, from Poland, and fluent in Spanish, Italian, and English (with a heavy accent), one of the first tasks he assigned to me, and another associate was census taking. Our mission was to visit every single parishioner and record the number of children and the religious status of each. This was a tough job, but it was also an excellent opportunity to get to know the people of the parish (and actually become a bit more proficient in my Spanish).

I met many young people through the census taking process, and immediately recognized the need for special activities geared toward their interests. I recalled the young associates who had done so much for the young people in the parish before I left for the seminary. That led me to decide that I must take up that challenge and bring back many of the youth who had joined a non-Catholic youth group several blocks from our parish.

Most of the parish young people attended the public high school that I had planned to attend, so we held religious classes for them once a week. Attendance was poor. I needed an activity, a magnet to draw the teenagers to these classes. With permission from the pastor, I converted the large hall under the church into a social hall. An old donated jukebox and the girls' popular records was tempting enough to have the boys attend the required religion classes held every Friday evening. The girls didn't mind the classes because they loved the socials. The boys, on the other hand, were not necessarily interested in religion classes they did attend mostly because of the opportunity to meet the girls. I monitored attendance at classes and served as the "bouncer" for the Friday Nite Socials. We sometimes had gang fights outside the hall, but I was usually able to get them to make peace (otherwise they could not join the dances). Eventually, the parish was also able to sponsor some organized sports, but that was a costly venture, and difficult to justify since our young people had the opportunity to become involved in the sports programs at school.

Another challenge during my first assignment was a teaching position in the local Catholic high school in our Hammond city area. The bishop of our diocese recruited the newly ordained priests working in his diocese for a year of teaching. I assume that my pastor chose me for this assignment because he felt that I needed the experience.

Those first years of my priesthood goal were busy and challenging ones. I learned through my mistakes, and a priest friend who shared advice with me based on the lessons of his own experience. I was very happy, yet I still desired to be in the military and serve in some capacity. Some of the young teenagers I had taught would eventually volunteer for some branch of the Military Service. I envied them in a way as I saw them standing straight and tall, transformed into young adults willing to serve their country. Yes, I had met challenges and attained goals, but I was still dreaming of one day wearing the uniform of the Armed Forces. Young Americans needed a Chaplain especially in combat.

As time passed, a new pastor was sent to my parish in Indiana. I had the strong feeling he did not take kindly to my popularity among the teenagers. In fact, he told me he did not like that there were teenagers in my office so often. I didn't pay much attention to him because I felt strongly that the teenagers needed attention.

Chapter 12:
The Southern Missions

Not long after the new pastor arrived, I received a letter from my superior, the Provincial, who informed me that I was to report to a mission parish in northern Mississippi. My desire to join the military, perhaps as a chaplain, increased as I faced this new assignment. Nevertheless, I packed my bags and headed south. Upon my arrival, I met the pastor (Father Paul) who to my delight was a priest who knew me and my entire family when he was pastor, and I was just a "Kid". He also built the church that I later served in as an associate. I was very happy to have him as my new boss because he was the priest I most often desired to emulate.

Father Paul, my new "boss" told me that he was assigning me to St. Mary's, the Black mission parish in Holly Springs, Mississippi. He had been responsible for building a new elementary and high school there and obtaining nuns (from Milwaukee, Wisconsin) to teach in the new school. The nuns were Franciscans and were very dedicated. They did so much and were always ready to do even more for the parishioners and students of Saint Mary's, the only Black Catholic school in northern Mississippi. I was to be in charge of the religious side of this mission and serve as the athletic director. In addition, I would be teaching Religion and American History. This sounded challenging to me, especially the part about being in charge. One wing of the long building served as the grade school, offices and a chapel. The other wing contained the high school classrooms plus a beautiful gymnasium. The new gym was used for many activities such as PTA meetings, school assemblies, contests, and graduations. I eventually initiated roller skating there for those who wished to socialize. This was certainly an appealing setup. My young couples loved it. The athletic coach told me that the school had an excellent basketball team, but when I asked about baseball and football, he told me they did not have the money for equipment or an athletic field. I remember responding emphatically and confidently, "Coach, I'll get you the equipment and build you an athletic field, you get me the teams!" In less than a year I collected enough used baseball and football uniforms and equipment from Chicago-area Catholic high schools while our coach "drafted" potential star football or baseball athletes. You may not believe this but within a year our high school took State Championship of all Black High Schools in Mississippi.

The reader should be aware that at this time in the South, racial discrimination was very much a central fact of life. Blacks had their own schools and churches, as well as specified places for sitting in the town's only theater. I witnessed rioting that took place in front of our school. On one occasion, college students from the North, for good or for bad, came down and joined the local Black students from the two Black colleges in town. They marched over to our school and began to demonstrate on our grounds. I knew they were there to stir up our students, so I ran down and advised them to get off our private property or get arrested. They asked me if I were Black or White. I replied that I was whatever they wanted me to be and that they had better march off quickly. Surprisingly, they left without any commotion. When our student body witnessed what had happened, a huge cheer came up from every classroom. The college students never bothered us again. In addition to this demonstration, I was there when we notified the students that President John F. Kennedy had been assassinated. And I was present to witness some of the senior students volunteering for military service, young people that I later encountered when I myself was in uniform. My few years working with the Black community in the South were very rewarding.

Chapter 13:
Volunteering for the Military

Once I reached my thirties, I realized that if I wanted to serve in the military, I must act promptly. I had made a series of requests to join the military, requests that were always turned down, so I approached my Superior. He also denied my request for military duty, asserting that there was a shortage of priests and he could not afford to let me go. I was not happy with his decision, but I was not discouraged. Our new superior general in Rome was an American and a person who listened, so I decided to write him a personal note explaining my long dream to serve in the military. He wrote back immediately, telling me that he could not go against my local superior's decision; however, he would suggest to him to reconsider. I later found out that the local provincial took a vote among his council members, and it was their vote that got me the permission I needed to volunteer for the military.

There were other hurdles to overcome before I could be accepted into the military. The first step was to go to the nearest recruiter in Chattanooga, Tennessee and sign up for the Navy. Although I wanted to work with the marines, it was required that chaplains desiring to serve with the Marines must become Navy Chaplains. The recruiter had never been approached by a clergyman, so he did not quite know what to do. When I gave him the completed forms, he noted that I had undergone a laminectomy (surgery on a disc) because of a football injury back in high school. This, he stated, did not matter. It was grounds for automatic disqualification. I tried to convince him that I was now in good physical condition and was willing to undergo any physical testing to prove that I was fit. That did not help, so I returned to Mississippi a bit dejected but not discouraged.

I then applied for the Air Force thinking that surely this branch would accept me. Again, I received the same response. I appealed to the Chief of Chaplains for the Air Force assuring him that I was willing to fly out to his office in San Antonio, Texas to undergo a physical exam under his supervision, but even he believed that "the law was the law." The Air Force wanted the best of the best. I still felt I must not give up on my dream despite these somewhat overwhelming obstacles.

Although the Army was the least appealing branch of military service to me, I felt I had to try again, so I flew up to Milwaukee on the advice of a former Army chaplain and approached a recruiter. For the third time I was told that the type of surgery I had undergone automatically disqualified me from acceptance into the military. This third rejection hit me like a ton of bricks, and I began to argue with the recruiter, assuring him, as I had done with previous recruiters, that I would undergo any physical exam to prove that I was fit.

A young doctor had been listening to us and he approached me saying, "You really want to join, don't you, reverend?" I replied, "With all my heart and soul." He then told me to sit down and wait. After what seemed like an eternity, he returned, and with hand extended, congratulated me. He had called the Army Chief of Surgeons in Washington DC and obtained a medical waiver for me. I let out a yell, "Thank you, God! Thank you, God!" The doctor told me that the other branches of the Services could have gotten a medical waiver just as he had. Perhaps your Boss wanted you with us"! It was not an impossible situation, as they had tried to convince me. Everything depended on my ability to "pass" every challenge dished out to me. "THAT'S ALL?", I said. Someday I would seek revenge!

Upon being approved, I still had to fill out more forms and answer more questions. One question was about what type of work I wanted to get involved in. At the time, a lot of recruiting was being done for the newly formed Army Special Forces. They were the elite branch of the Army. My "I'll show them" attitude resurfaced as I thought of the other services telling me I could not handle their tough training. Without hesitation, I printed in large, bold letters: SPECIAL FORCES. Weeks later I was notified that the Army's Chief of Chaplains had accepted my application, and the Department of the Army mailed me my first set of orders. I was assigned to the 3rd Special Forces Group located at Ft Bragg, North Carolina, after first completing the basic chaplain's course.

Chapter 14:
Chaplain School &Army Special Forces

At the chaplain's school I met ministers from many denominations, all eager to serve God and country. On the very first day at Fort Hamilton, we were given our uniforms and taught how to pin or sew the different insignia onto our uniform blouse. They also taught us how to stand tall, an easy task for me since I was so proud of my new position and uniform. A Lutheran chaplain who was also assigned to Special Forces, as well as having had prior enlisted time, and coincidentally from the same hometown I was raised in East Chicago, Indiana, helped me with the uniform and showed me how to put on the Green Beret the distinctive headgear of Special Forces.

Subjects in the classes to which we were assigned included military history, military etiquette, counseling, and a clinical pastoral education course, how to salute, how to march. Much emphasis was given to the physical aspect of our training. The Vietnam War was in progress, and without question we would all be involved in it. Training included live fire, firing an M-15, grenade throwing, land navigation, and time in a gas chamber—we were doing everything that the young enlisted soldier did in preparation for combat. The instructors at the chaplain's school were for the most part experienced combat chaplains. They transmitted to us the tools for success and dedication to duty that prepared us for the difficult job they knew so well.

Upon graduation, we were given our orders to transfer immediately to our official assignment. I reported to the 3rd Special Forces Group Headquarters at Fort Bragg North Carolina, and felt a sense of kinship almost immediately even though I still had a great deal of training to undergo. The senior chaplain in the Group, a major in rank, was very helpful and went out of his way to make sure I mingled with the men. The Group at the time had the unusual task of training young enlistees as they went through basic training for the regular Army. It was my job to give the character guidance classes to these young men. In preparation for this, my mentor chaplain had me go through a "Dry Run" by giving my talk to him in an empty auditorium. I felt transported back to the long-ago days when I was a young seminarian, but I appreciated his help and advice.

A few weeks after settling in at Fort Bragg, personnel called me and told me to prepare for airborne training at Ft. Benning, Georgia. I had been expecting this move, and in fact had voluntarily been physically conditioning myself long before I was accepted into the military. Physical exercises and jogging were part of my daily routine even when I was at St. Mary's in Mississippi. I regularly joined my school athletes as their coach ran them through rigorous physical training So, with this background of physical preparation, it was with great anticipation and excitement that I departed for Fort Benning.

Chapter 15:
Airborne Training

Fort Benning, Georgia, was and still is the home of the airborne. I was scared but curious as to how I would do in this training. I was thirty-six years old, while all the other students were only in their late teens or early twenties. Even the other officers in airborne training were younger than me. This would be a challenge!

We were herded into WW II type barracks with rows of bunk beds and wooden footlockers for storing our belongings. We had fatigues, boots, and one dress uniform. All these items had to be perfectly starched, and pressed, with the boots "spit-shined". Our beds had to always be made in military fashion. We were warned about the length of our hair, so we all had the shortest haircuts possible.

Officers and enlisted men in the basic training course, were all volunteers. A rigorous physical test was required before we were sent for this training. The BAC consisted of three weeks of intensive instruction and was the most physically demanding experience that I had ever volunteered for. Daily runs in the early morning followed by physical exercises such as well as jumps from mock up airplane doors, and jumps from a tower that seemed to reach the sky (with an already open parachute foto on the left).

The instructors, (or "black hats" as we called them,) were highly trained and motivated non-commissioned officers whose task it was to make us Airborne qualified (out of a perfectly good airplane). No preferential treatment was given to the officers or the chaplains. Initially I dreaded seeing the black hats during training because I knew that inevitably one would yell out to me, "DROP! DROP!" This dropping onto the gravel and doing ten pushups or more was "torture". To this day, I can still see the instructor's face and his steely, mean looking eyes, smell his cigar breath, and hear his voice booming out at me.

(DROP, CHAPPIE, DROP!" Now, however, I know that all the harassment was done for a reason. It developed muscles on my arms and back, muscles that helped me maneuver the parachute. The long, endless runs, plus the sit-ups, pull resulted in me successfully making the five required parachute jumps from a perfectly good airplane.

During the entire training I was both scared and worried about making it. Many, many good, physically fit young trainees were dropped from the course because of injury or because the instructor felt the soldier was not ready. There were also those soldiers who dropped out on their own volition. An opportunity was given to some to repeat the training. I swore to myself that I would not repeat—NO WAY!

During jump week, however, I did not make a proper parachute landing fall on my fourth jump, so I woke up on the final jump day with a swollen thigh. (I could barely walk), but I made it to the hall for the final briefing. One of the instructors noticed my limp and recommended that I go to the medic. I told him I was fine, that I would make the jump, and that I would graduate. He just shook his head and said: "All right, Chappie, get on the bus with the others!"

The proudest day of my new life in the military was when those silver wings were pinned on my chest by none other than the black hat who most loved to make me do pushups! I was airborne-qualified—I was a paratrooper! I was doubly proud when I was told that I had orders waiting for me back at Fort Bragg. I hoped the orders would direct me to the Special Forces Qualification (the "Q" Course) that was a requirement for working with and for this elite group, and for wearing the coveted Green Beret. The Q-Course was one of the most physically demanding courses. Once completed, a soldier was fully qualified to wear the Green Beret with the flash that signified to which of the five groups one was assigned. Upon my return to Fort Bragg, North Carolina, I was given orders to report to the First Special Forces based on Okinawa) located on Okinawa, where I would also be given the opportunity to qualify for SF assignments.

Chapter 16:
Okinawa.

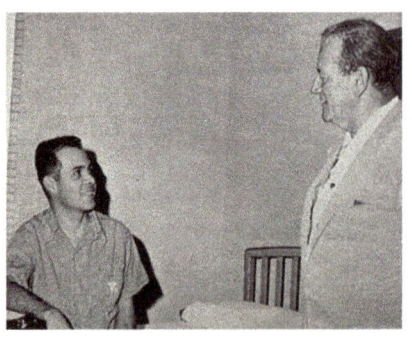

After taking a 30-Day leave before heading overseas, I arrived at Kadena Air Force Base on Okinawa. Upon arriving, I reported to Special Forces Headquarters, but when the head Army chaplain met me, he told me that he was having my orders changed and I would be reassigned to the Army hospital. He had changed my orders. I felt the blood shooting up to my head. "Sir," I said, "My orders come from our Chief of Chaplains who personally promised me that, whenever possible, I would be trained and assigned to Special Forces units. If this is the way the Army does things, I will immediately resign my commission!" I then went back to my commander and explained the incident. "Don't worry Padre, I'll cut the new orders, but only to give you an additional duty at the Army hospital. You will still officially be our Special Forces chaplain." I didn't know that he was the officer who had the authority to cut orders for me. Well, how about that? I felt that I was right in expressing my feelings, and that God was certainly at my side. I knew that the hospital commander was demanding that his chaplain's slot be filled, and the senior chaplain believed he could easily change my orders. One of the highlights of my tour in Okinawa was when I was a patient in the hospital my favorite movie star John Wayne. He was on Okinawa in search of a place where he would film his movie "Green Beret". This assignment to the 1st Special Forces Group was definitely the best assignment for me. The men treated me with respect and did everything they could to see that I performed my duties. They noticed that my beret had only a candy stripe instead of the flash, so they began encouraging and challenging me to begin studying and preparing for the big test, the passing of which would allow me to wear the flash. The lower rank candy stripe was an embroidered one-half inch by two-inch bar with the Groups colors' bar sewn on the beret, as opposed to the shield shaped one designating the group to which one belonged.

I traveled on temporary duty to other countries—Thailand, Korea and Japan. My men challenged me to get SCUBA qualified because they were involved in scuba training and wanted their chaplain to participate in the graduations held underwater. Part of this training involved exiting from air locks in a submarine and infiltrating enemy territory. I felt CLAUSTROPHOBIC under water, leading me to realize why I had never been drawn to submarine duty.

The next challenge was what we call "HALO" This was one of the specialties of Special Forces teams—they had to always be prepared to infiltrate by jumping from unbelievably high altitudes in special parachutes with full equipment. Once again, I was scared to death the first time, I jumped from over five thousand feet. The island of Okinawa seemed like a speck from that height, and I feared I would land in the water miles away; however, I did have deep faith in the men who did the parachute rigging and the Jump Master so, once in the air, I began to enjoy the high-altitude jumps. It was so peaceful and quiet as we floated down.

Because our Group's mission was also to train and prepare Green Berets for a tour, we also trained them in SCUBA (under water missions) the trainers thought I should also be qualified and participate in graduating ceremonies so how could I refuse. I never really looked forward to those graduation ceremonies (very honestly because I was deathly afraid of being attacked by some shark).

The final portion of training with the 1st Special Forces Group was to march through the jungle from one end of the island to the other. Tough mission if you lost faith in your instructors. Aside from the military training with my unit, I also helped other Catholic chaplains with Sunday services, religious education for family members, and other spiritual ministries.

In Vietnam there were approximately 111 A-Teams in the 5th Special Forces Group scattered throughout the country, and they were divided into four parts (I Corps, II Corps, III Corps and IV Corps). Special Forces has a different configuration than that of a regular Army unit. The basic unit of a Special Forces group is the twelve-man A detachment or A-Team. The A-Team consists of ten well-trained men in two MOS's. It is commanded by a captain, and the executive officer is a first lieutenant or Warrant Officer. Each man is cross-trained and speaks at least one language other than English. In addition to the A-Teams, there are B Teams that make up the next step. These are primarily support and administrative in nature. The final organizational division is C, a Battalion headquarters. I felt that I was qualified to be one of the five chaplains assigned to 5th Special Forces Group.

Chapter 17:
IV Corps, Vietnam

It was luck, determination, and a friendship with the Army Chief of Chaplains, Major General Francis Sampson (who was a paratrooper of World War II fame), that got me the assignment to the 5th Special Forces Group in Vietnam. I think that I was the only qualified Special Forces priest available at the time. Whatever the reason, I received my orders and traveled to Vietnam. When I arrived, I thought that all I had to do was to report to Special Forces Headquarters, so I went directly there. I was surprised, therefore, when I got an urgent notice from the Military Command Vietnam (MACV) chaplains' office in Saigon to report to them ASAP.

Upon arriving there, I was reprimanded and told that my orders were changed and that I was to go to Can Tho in the Mekong River Delta area to serve as the 4th Corps Senior Chaplain. Never one to take things lying down, I argued, telling them that I had special orders from the Chief of Chaplains himself, and that those orders assigned me to the 5th Special Forces Group. I could not argue too much because, after all, I was still just a 1st Lieutenant while the chaplains I was addressing were colonels. I finally agreed to go down to the Delta if they would consider eventually sending me to Special Forces where I belonged. They conceded. My assignment was to replace a priest in Can Tho who had been in the country for a year, so it didn't take him long to catch a flight to Saigon and then home.

The day after my arrival I became familiar with the compound and made friends with an American civilian who worked for Catholic Charities in the town. He and I spent the day driving around the town of Can Tho, and I learning about his work and the need for mutual cooperation. Throughout the entire day I felt a certain uneasiness though, especially how our Vietnamese counterparts were nervously acting. At one point, just on the outskirts of town, we were stopped by Vietnamese guards and advised to return to our compound. It was "TET" the Vietnamese holiday, their National New Year and they knew the Vietcong were planning something.

Most of our living quarters were small huts made of cinder block, pieces of lumber, and sometimes a cement floor. I had only been asleep for a short while when I was awakened by loud explosive noises and the shattering of glass. It did not take long for me to figure out: the celebrations had now begun. Putting on my helmet and armored vest, and with my catholic chaplain's blessed oils I looked for a place where I might be of help. No one seemed to know where that might be, so I headed to the soccer field which was being used as a landing place for helicopters bringing in the wounded and the dying. I anointed or prayed over the injured and dying soldiers. This was my" baptism by fire," and it went on all night. It didn't take me long to realize that I was now involved. I was responsible for Catholic coverage in isolated sites as well where there was no chaplain. In order to visit all of these sites, a Protestant chaplain and I were usually provided with aircraft, either helicopter or fixed wing. On Sundays we spent all day flying from camp to camp. It was not unusual to celebrate five or six services on a Sunday. We became known as the "Delta Chaplains". I came to rather enjoy the flying and ministering to the troops stationed out in the "boonies," far from anything familiar, but I still longed for the day when I would be shipped up to "my Home" with Special Forces and 5th Special Forces Group Headquarters. In the meantime, I continued to work in Can Tho and out of that same Soccer field. It was not very long before I felt that I was a veteran. More than ever, I appreciated the spirit and bravery of our young American soldiers. They inspired me!

Chapter 18:
Special Forces, Vietnam.

A few months after my arrival in southern Vietnam, I finally got the orders that would join me with my men, the Special Forces soldiers. Almost immediately upon my arrival and introduction the commander, I could see that the men accepted me as one of their own. The commander already knew me from Okinawa, and he realized how much I longed to be with Special Forces. I had also worked under the senior chaplain stationed there while I was in Okinawa, so it was like being home again. In addition to the senior chaplain, there were four other chaplains, two Catholic and two Protestant, and we were assigned to one of the four Corps on a rotational basis. During the month we spent with each corps, we visited every A-Team site, delivered mail and care packages, and counseled and offered religious services. Every two weeks we could return to headquarters to do our laundry, pick up our mail, and just rest for a day before heading out to the field again.

Our brief visits to the A-Team sites, two days at most, depended on the availability of transportation. We literally hitched a ride by helicopter to every location. This was good for the team members, as they at least got to see a new face on a somewhat regular basis. I remember one young captain in particular who was small in stature, but built like a horse. Everyone called him "Hoss" because of his toughness and bravado. He initially did not take to me because, I believe, he was uncomfortable around me. "I don't need no religion and chaplain to get me to go to church," he would say. One day he and his team were out on an operation with their counterparts, and they were mistaken by a gunship helicopter as the enemy so the pilots dove down and began firing at "Hoss" and his men. "Hoss" jumped up from the tall elephant grass cursing and swearing; then he shocked everyone by making the sign of the cross on his forehead. Miraculously, the gunships flew off. As for

"Hoss", he was heard shouting, "God is alive and doing well!" That evening he attended my Mass and even received communion.

Another incident which I will never forget was a memorial service I held at a compound in Da Nang. The compound had been mortared and infiltrated in the middle of the night, and we lost at least four Americans and several Vietnamese. I had never witnessed such devotion and reverence as I did at that service, and no funeral since then has surpassed the depth of emotion. The term "Band of Brothers" is often used today, but believe me, this bond has always existed in times of combat. I once had a sergeant die in my arms. His buddies openly wept while I administered the last rites. He was truly loved by his team.

New and difficult challenges continued to confront me. There was, for example, a certain major who emphasized to his men that I would be conducting Mass upon my arrival and expected a good attendance. He also always invited me to walk around the perimeter of his camp, knowing full well that the enemy was watching. I felt he was either testing me, or proving to his men that if the chaplain could do it, so could anyone else.

On another occasion, this same major asked me to accompany him as he drove his Jeep around the camp's perimeter to check out the security on a road he was having built. He handed me an M16 and told me to serve as "point man" as he drove (and I marched in front of his jeep in complete darkness). I really believed I would be shot then and there since the enemy was in the vicinity. I also thought the major was crazy, but I was not about to show him that I was frightened to death. Upon our return to camp, I reverently thanked the good Lord for His protection. Weeks later, the major and his sergeant were killed as they surveyed that very same area.

These incidents involving my foolishness and the major's challenge did, however, earn me the respect of the men under his command. I must also add that I certainly was no braver or better than other chaplains during combat. I was only grateful that I was fortunate enough to receive the training I did prior to going into combat.

Although they were well defended, the Special Forces camps were small, and were subject to many attacks at night, so the entire perimeter was always heavily surrounded by barbed wire and empty coke or beer cans as a warning that intruders were approaching. Many of the men slept in underground bunks they had dug out. The central gathering place was the team house or bar. This was usually the best place for the chaplain to hang out since men not on an operation usually congregated there, drinking or listening to music. This was usually the place where I held my religious service. Although I initially felt uncomfortable because of the many *"PLAYBOY" center folds* posted on the walls, I gradually came to believe that the faith of the soldiers was what counted.

If I had to stay overnight at one of the A-Team camps, one of the men always found a bunk for me. In fact, movie star Martha Raye traveled in much the same way as I did, (except that she always had an escort to protect her). She was quite the gal and was loved by every single Green Beret. I came to enjoy telling the story of our encounters as we traveled the country while she was visiting us. She and I often shared the same bunk during our visits (but at different times, of course). She would arrive when I was preparing to leave, or she would be departing just as I was arriving. She learned that I carried a bunch of religious medals made especially for the Airborne, so inevitably she would take whatever I had to give to the men, and I would have to get another supply when I returned to Nha Trang. Years later I called her at her home in Beverly Hills while on leave in San Diego, and she talked me into visiting her. She had dozens of appreciation plaques that were presented to her while on her visits to troops in Vietnam. We talked about our visits to the Green Beret Camps and delighted in our shared memories. Our reunion visit lasted until the wee hours of the morning when I finally departed and began the drive back to San Diego.

Another clear Vietnam memory was made while I was visiting a B Company Commander and his men located in Bien Hoa. I had not even been assigned a bunk when the commander, a Catholic, invited me to accompany him and his first sergeant in a helicopter as they "reconned" an area where Vietcong were thought to be infiltrating. We were not up for more than ten minutes when our helicopter suddenly stalled and we had to "auto-gyrate" onto a rice paddy, making us literally sitting ducks. The colonel glanced over at me and asked if I had a weapon. When I told him that chaplains were non-combatants and forbidden to carry a weapon, according to the Geneva Convention he reached into his side pocket, handed me a 45MM, and commented "Geneva be damned. Use this when you have to." He then had us form a perimeter around our chopper while the pilot radioed back to headquarters requesting help. For what seemed like hours, we waited in silence, expecting at any minute to be ambushed. I prayed and prayed deeply, sincerely, for protection. God was definitely with us; no enemy came near us before another chopper and mechanic arrived to help us get back to the compound. I did not know it at the time, but I later learned that the commander had a son who was studying for the priesthood. Some years later I met his son who had become a priest and an Army chaplain. God works in mysterious ways!

While on one of my visits to a camp near the Cambodian border, I tried getting a ride back to another A-Team site but was told that there was no helicopter available, except for one whose passengers were two captured prisoners (POWs) If I was willing to serve as their escort, I could fly out with them. So, suddenly I found myself with two Vietcong prisoners, sitting next to me some three or four thousand feet over the jungle with the doors wide open. Would they dare jump me or push me over the side? I decided to try communicating with them through a form of sign language sprinkled with a few Vietnamese words. When I finally thought to offer them each a cigarette, a smile broke out on their faces. At last, I felt safe, or as safe as one could be in those circumstances.

I had further interaction with the Vietnamese through one of the Group Commanders I met during my first tour; a colonel known by everyone as "Iron Mike". He was the epitome of a true, experienced Special Forces Commander. Iron Mike seemed to know every senior officer at MACV (Military Assistance C0mmand Vietnam), as well as their Vietnamese counterparts. He was also acquainted with the native clergy and was always doing favors for them. I personally got involved when he helped the clergy. On a number of occasions, one of the AIR AMERICA helicopters or fixed wing aircraft would fly me to some part of the country to pick up a bishop. Through such socializing and granting favors, the "Colonel" obtained vital information that helped to our operations. Iron Mike was a native of Chicago and upon retiring he returned to the Windy City and went to work for the police department.

My two tours with Special Forces in Vietnam made me admire the dedication and bravery of the men in the Green Beret. They were professionals who had a mission and completed it with a passion. I was their chaplain when the 5th Special Forces Group received orders to return the colors back to Fort Bragg, and I quoted ST Paul's Second Letter to Timothy (replacing "I" with "you") when they boarded the planes for their return trip to the US: "You have fought the good fight, you have finished the race, you have kept the faith."

For the remainder of my second tour, I stayed on as chaplain to the men left behind who were referred to as the men of the Training Support Headquarters ("TISH)" or ironically calling ourselves "The Brave Men With the Baseball Caps" This contingent of ex-Special Forces soldiers continued to train Vietnamese, Montagnard, and Cambodian soldiers. Green Berets were traded for baseball caps and the men weren't happy, but they had a mission to perform. And they never disappointed.

Chapter 19:
A Tour With The 82nd Airborne Division

After the completion of my second Vietnam tour and a thirty-day leave, I reported to my new assignment in Fort Bragg, North Carolina, as chaplain to the 4th Battalion 325th Airborne Infantry Regiment of the famed 82nd Airborne. I thought I would have time to relax; however, I soon discovered that we were always on alert, and always had to have a packed rucksack stored in our chapel storage room. We could and were called at any hour of the day or night and bussed to the Tarmac at Pope Air Force Base adjacent to our 82nd Airborne Division and wait, wait for the alert order to "Fly and Jump" out of a "perfectly" good, well-built C-141.

Many were the alerts, but few were the actual departures. The purpose was to be prepared, so I knew I had to be in even better physical condition. I also enjoyed the opportunity to continue parachute jumps. During this tour I was able to earn my Master Parachutist Wings! It was also during this time that I decided to take flying lessons and completed my solo. I used to think, God, this Army life is my cup of tea. I've become a priest, and now a chaplain in the military. What more can I ask for?

Chapter 20:
10th Special Forces.

Through the grapevine, I learned that the 10th SPECIAL Forces GROUP was in need of a qualified Catholic chaplain, so I immediately began to write to individuals and asked for an inter-theatre transfer. I knew the senior chaplain of the group, so with his influence, I was soon given orders to report to Bad Toelz, Germany. It is located in the Bavarian Alps and is one of the most scenic locations I have ever been to. How could I not be happy with what I was doing and where I was going? The Post (Military Kaserne) had been a former German Military installation surrounded by dense forests and beautiful Pine covered tops. The local people seemed to love the Americans and the good relationship was mutual. During our training in unconventional warfare, the townsfolk joyfully played an active role. It was very similar to the Q-Course training back at Fort Bragg.

The commander, Colonel Ludwig Faistenhammer, with whom I had served in Vietnam and who had coincidently been born in Bavaria, was loved by his own, and respected by the Americans. Because he was a disciplinarian and excellent leader, we called him "Mad Max". I recall a number of occasions during our regular Friday morning inspections when he caught me needing a haircut, or needing to spit-shine my boots, or not having any "patch" on my uniform properly sewn (according to his standards). He would drop me for pushups and fine me a few dollars to be donated to the chapel (not to me) But he did this to all the troops, officer and NCO alike, so we all respected him.

The 10th Special Forces Group conducted wonderful training, and I loved it. We did HALO, standard land and water jumps, as well as scuba training in Finland, France, Italy, Spain, and Greece. We cross-country skied in the mountains of Bavaria, and conducted field training exercises. Since family members lived with us, I had a regular parish ministry with wives and children. Whenever possible I tried to go on temporary duty to visit teams who were out of country.

I once visited our scuba team in Cartagena, Spain, where we were training their sailors how to "water jump". One of my young Lieutenants, (perhaps attempting to befriend these Navy Guys) volunteers me. I was to SCUBA dive for them so they could have a replacement of their stolen statue Mary and replaced with a new one. The Spanish sailors had inquired of my men whether they had a Scuba qualified Catholic Chaplain who might be SUBA qualified. Well..., leave it to one of a Lieutenant buddy to tell them that the US Army could provide the Navy with their Catholic Chaplain. Well.... I've never enjoyed being "volunteered"; I prefer volunteering on my own. But, (I nervously borrowed some Scuba equipment, carried a jug of holy water to bless the new statue, and followed the Spanish sailors down into a bay. Propped up in a huge cave with a narrow opening was a beautiful statue of Mary. I didn't feel too badly after I blessed and placed the statue on a firm strong pedestal.

On another occasion, after returning from Spain I jumped with our scuba team over Lake Starnberg in Bavaria. We jumped in groups, from helicopters so when my turn came, I waited, waited, and waited some more, wondering why my entire group had reached the water, while I couldn't I even descend an inch. I was still "hanging" up in the skies physically unable to descend I floated for what like seemed forever. I really think I began to panic because I heard my men yelling up at me to pull the risers to partially deflate the chute. Thought they were kidding while they laughed aloud. I had been caught in an "Air Pocket". I think about that incident, and many more, and just shake my head thinking, it was fun then! (Especially when my men joked about God wanting to keep me "UP There!".

Toward the end of my three-year tour in Germany, I learned that the US ARMY Chief Chaplain offered priests the opportunity to take a theology renewal course at the Pontifical North American College in Rome (just behind the Vatican). There was an opening for one chaplain, so I immediately applied feeling I had nothing to lose. Three months on temporary duty, living as a civilian and enjoying the eternal city! The good Lord was on my side again and I was given orders. to go. What an opportunity! And it wasn't going to personally cost me a cent. And I would even get to meet Pope John! I came, I saw, and I conquered.

After three months of living a civilian student life the time arrived for me to return to my USA.

Chapter 21:
Command & General Staff College

Reporting to an Army surrounding atmosphere, was like a homecoming of sorts. because I had been born in Salina, just several miles away. Ft Leavenworth is what many soldiers refer to as a "Lifers College" Though established primarily for "line officers" who will lead battalions, brigades and Divisions, some chaplains are also chosen since they too must understand the system. I had spent my entire career serving with the unconventional Special Forces organization, so learning the conventional Army structure was necessary for me to continue being a chaplain. I graduated successfully and was assigned to the School Brigade at Fort Benning, Georgia. Again, I have to confess, I was being blessed with excellent assignments. I ministered to future Army officers, future Military leaders, and Airborne troopers.

Chapter 22:
Germany and the 1st Infantry Division

My next assignment was the First Infantry Division located in Goepingen Germany, located just south of Stuttgart but still in the Bavarian section of the country. The First Infantry, or the" BIG RED ONE" as it is better known, is located in a very industrialized area and in a former Nazi Kaserne. The Big Red One unit trained in areas such as Graffenwoer and Wildflicken, and like the 82nd Airborne Division back in the US, training was always ongoing. In fact, we trained for so long and for such distances that my mode of travel was a quarter-ton pickup truck. I found an old Volkswagon Van in the Base's Vehicle dump, cut the top half so that it fit snugly onto my Army issued "pickup", furnished the cab with wooden paneling, added two benches which served as cots, camouflaged it, and "voila!", I called it the" CHAPMOBILE". I didn't feel too badly living out in fields during the cold German Winter…. My Protestant Chaplain envied me.

About midway through my tour, I was moved up to the VII Corps Headquarters as Deputy Corps Chaplain. I began to realize that the higher up one gets in rank as an officer, the further removed one can get from the young soldiers, so I vowed that I would never allow that to happen to me. They were the only reason why I was happy. However, "THY WILL BE DONE"!

While stationed in Stuttgart, I approached 25 years of ordination to the priesthood, my Silver Jubilee. Where had all those years gone? The commanding general and the entire community arranged for a special celebration in our "Club", after which I was granted leave to return to the US to celebrate with family and friends.

Chapter 23:
From Fort Benning to Carlisle Barracks

After completing my tour in Germany, I received orders to report to Fort Benning, Georgia (my old stomping ground) The senior chaplain would be retiring so he appointed me as his successor. I became the command chaplain for the entire post. I was delighted because this was the home of the Officer Candidate School, the Infantry School, the Airborne School, and Ranger School. As senior chaplain, I was responsible for providing chaplains and chaplain assistants for all units. Since I was now the boss, I felt that I could continue working for the young soldiers, and I could cover almost any unit I wanted to without any complaints. My favorite people to minister to were the airborne, the rangers, and of course, the Special Forces.

Much to my surprise, I was notified one day that I had been chosen to attend the prestigious War College located in the rolling plains of Central Kansas. The courses were geared toward preparing senior military officers, and included lectures on topics such as strategy, politics, and leadership. Usually only one or two chaplains are picked for each year's class, and I really felt blessed and honored to be selected. Our class was divided into sections, and included officers from the Navy and Marines, as well as foreign officers from Latin America, Saudi Arabia, and England. We frequently had guest speakers from the US Department of Justice, as well as instructional visits from general officers. We were also able to take several trips as part of our studies as well as a realistic Field Exercise. I have included two fotos of the prestigious Army Colleges not to really brag but to show that my "Be All You Can Be" attitudes certainly were rewarding.

Chapter 24:
Panama

After graduation from the War College at Ft. Leavenworth I received orders for Panama to be the chaplain for the US Southern Command and US Army South. I never dreamed being selected for the senior position in Panama, but it was probably because our country's leaders knew that our future relationship with Panama's military leader would be difficult, and felt that a chaplain who spoke Spanish and happened to be Catholic was a good idea. The assignment sounded exciting and challenging, and I was anxious to go.

Headquarters was located right beside the famous "Panama Canal" and had everything a military installation in the US would have—family housing, exchange, commissary, chapel, hospital, and athletic fields. US Southern Command Headquarters, which was made up of officers from all branches of the military (Army, Navy, Air Force, Marines) and civilian agencies, was located a few miles closer to Panama City. On the Atlantic side of the Canal, we had the 8th Special Forces Group whose primary mission was to operate in other Latin American countries. "What a Life!"

The young, aggressive Brigadier General was an exciting individual. I think he took to me because he knew I was then the oldest colonel in his command, and he would challenge me in PT (physical training) every morning. As head chaplain, I had the opportunity to accompany him to other countries, and since many religious leaders were Catholic, and I spoke Spanish, we got along. My commanding general also knew full well that with a Catholic chaplain at his side, he would fare well in the eyes of the Latin-American Military. Toward the end of my tour in Panama, I learned that my next assignment was Ft. Devens, Mass. However, this would never materialize. To prepare for my return to the US, I spent an entire day in my quarters making sure that the movers packed all my household goods into crates and to be taken to a warehouse for shipment to CONUS (the continental US). I was fatigued by the end of the day, so after a sandwich and coke I went to bed on a cot I had borrowed. In spite of the uncomfortable cot, around midnight I was awakened by a large blast and machine gun fire just below my empty living room. I jumped out of bed, looked out my window, and saw an APC (armored personnel carrier) with our soldiers firing into the jungle directly across from my empty quarters. JUST CAUSE had begun. I had not even been briefed!

I instinctively put on my uniform and dashed down a street toward the main post chapel, where I was able to find uniform, a helmet and Catholic Oils for anointing of the wounded and dying... (mostly the 82 Abn troops who had just arrived from Fort Bragg. Eventually, a few of my chaplains and chaplain assistants came in and we set up a kind of center for troops passing by who needed a place to rest. My thoughts were with our wounded, so I went up the hill to our clinic and offered assistance. When I contacted Gorgas US Army hospital (a miles from our location). I was informed that there were no chaplains available because the military police would not allow them to leave their quarters. I "pirated" a Humvee, and ordered my driver to race, (like a bat out of hell), to the hospital where I remained all night and the following day ministering to the dying. During the day the hospital chaplains were allowed to leave their quarters and report to the hospital.

Upon my return to Fort Clayton, I was told by the new commanding general, Marc Cisneros, that we had Panama's president and vice president with their families in safe houses on our compound. He asked me to minister to them until they were flown out of country. The general also asked me to make contact with Panama's Archbishop McGrath, as well as the papal Nuncio who had given Noriega a place temporarily stay.

Since my replacement knew very little about the situation in Panama, General Cisneros asked me to consider remaining on his staff as his special advisor. Again, I felt that the Good Lord had a say in this because the Chief of Chaplains in Washington, DC, extended my tour, and as special advisor to the General, I became more involved with civic action and the Catholic charities of Panama. I ministered to Panama's President and family sheltered at a Ft Clayton" Safe House". I ministered to the Panamanian POWs This involved visiting local communities and communicating with leaders of the newly formed government, as well as Catholic church leaders. I did more civic action during my six-month extension than I had ever done before with Special Forces. During this time, one of my brothers who worked for the Central Intelligence Agency (CIA) was also transferred here with his family, so occasionally I relished a good home-cooked meal.

Chapter 25:
From Texas to Colorado

After my extended tour, I received orders from the Chief's office assigning me as Fifth Army chaplain with headquarters at Fort Sam Houston in Texas. As chaplain, I was responsible for the recruitment and training of chaplains for the Army's Active Duty and the Reserve components in approximately seven states in the West. This involved extensive traveling to the many training facilities, but it was a challenging and rewarding job. Operation "Desert Storm", the conflict in the Middle East began during this time, and it was my responsibility to recruit, recall, and assign chaplains to units deploying overseas. I wished that I could go back into action with the young soldiers.

After Desert Storm, I received orders assigning me as post chaplain for the home of the 4th Infantry Division based at. Fort Carson, Colorado Located some one hundred miles south of Denver, it was surrounded by beautiful mountains and plenty of territory for training. I was pleased to go there, first of all because it was an infantry division with plenty of young men and women eager to become soldiers, and secondly, I learned that a Special Forces unit would soon be arriving, and that construction of their facilities was underway. I looked forward to working with my kind of people once again.

As it turned out again, because of the Catholic chaplain shortage, I was regularly invited to minister to the Catholic soldiers out in the field. During my time there, the chaplains' section took over a cabin facility and used it as a retreat center where chaplains could hold religious retreats and conferences for their soldiers. Since it was located around ten miles from the main post, I felt we needed a special area in the middle of the division which could serve as an "Oasis" for soldiers at the end of a long day of training. One of the commanders offered me a brick building in the perfect location. It was like a United Service Organizations (USO) facility, and the soldiers loved it. I named it "INTERLUDE. "

My time for mandatory retirement was fast approaching, and I began to wonder what the future would be like. I planned to first take a "Sabbatical" (a one-year rest period), and then decide what type of job to ask for. You see, Catholic priests really don't retire, they just operate at different locations.

In February of 1995, I was given a tremendous ceremony and banquet. The 4th Infantry soldiers, and their band made me proud. Best of all, the Special Forces unit joined in the celebration. They all "made my day". I thought of the scripture quote I had used when the 5th Special Forces Group left Vietnam, and how it now applied to me: "I have fought the good fight, I have finished the race, I have kept the faith." I knew I could not separate myself completely from association with the military though, as you will see.

Chapter 26:
Arlington

Upon my retirement, I packed my belongings and drove to San Diego, California, where I intended to live with my mother and a brother. It took an effort to get adjusted, and it wasn't long before I got a surprise call from a very good chaplain friend of mine. Chaplain Willie Peacock. He had been my "Deputy" back in Texas. "Willie" was responsible for chaplains in the Fort Meyer area. He asked me whether I would be interested in working as the Catholic chaplain for Arlington National Cemetery. I would be on contract, and, even though retired, I would wear my uniform when "on Duty I would be able to wear a uniform while performing the burial ceremonies for the military personnel. I was stunned, but overjoyed! Because I had been given a year off from any duties. (Meaning I was kind of my own boss), SO…. I shouted: "Ok, Willie, when do I start?

After approval from Washington, I packed my bags and drove across the country from San Diego to Washington DC. And report for Duty, once again. It turned out that this assignment at Arlington was perhaps one of the most inspiring and rewarding of practically all of the assignments I ever had while on active duty. During my previous entire time in assignments, never, never would I have asked for this assignment. Every day I worked alongside young male and female soldiers the "Honor Guard", who took their job seriously and performed with the highest respect for fallen soldiers. These young men and women are the best of the best. Their uniforms are immaculate, their shoes had a "mirror-like" shine, and they marched ramrod straight. It was one of these young soldiers who encouraged me to put my experiences down in writing, and that is why you are reading this book. Six months after this rewarding assignment, my religious superior decided that I should return to civilian life so I bid farewell to a great bunch of young, dedicated soldiers. I felt uneasy with the move because I was never really told what my next assignment was. My now civilian superior was sending me as chaplain to an Indian School in Chamberlain, South Dakota. But it changed before I even departed from Arlington. Instead, I was told that I would be assigned to a parish in Texas. Oh Well!!!!!!!!!

Chapter 27:
Civilian Assignments

I drove from Virginia to Houston, Texas, with my station wagon packed to the ceiling. Upon arriving at the address, I had been given, I realized that I had been assigned to an inner-city parish, and it seemed like a good challenge. In just a few days I noticed the vast difference between civilian and military life. I was used to discipline and order, and always knowing what my mission was in the military. In civilian life, I felt I had to continue asking the pastor what he wanted me to do, what my mission was. Nonetheless, I gradually adapted and got involved with the various activities in the parish. I volunteered to work with the teenagers of the parish since that age group had consistently been my favorite throughout my priestly ministry.

After half a year of associate work in Texas, I decided it was time for me to reward my mother for all that she had done for me, so I sought to be "Incardinated" i.e., Separation from the Congregation of the Priests of the Sacred Heart and become a diocesan priest in the diocese of San Diego where my mother and a brother lived. The bishop accepted me into the diocese of San Diego, which meant that my mother was able to live with me after my brother died and didn't have to worry about anything—I was able to take care of her. I worked as a senior associate pastor for a rewarding ten years until I reached seventy.

My first job in the diocese was as an assistant to the pastor of St John the Evangelist Church and School in Encinitas, just north of San Diego. I immediately felt at home because of the Irish pastor, who allowed me to pursue ideas for improving the church as well as the new grade school he was building. The parish served a large Hispanic community, and he was an Irishman with no knowledge of Spanish so off I went to Encinitas. Assigned to work with the great monsignor, a truly great Pastor. I loved him because, every Saturday evening, after hearing confessions, he would invite me to a hearty dinner in one of the local seaside restaurants. My new life turned out to be "AOK"!

After about two years, I was transferred and made pastor of the Holy Family and grade school in "Chula Vista" My assistant and I provided services for the English, Hispanic, Filipino, Vietnamese, and Nhung communities. It seemed that my challenges were increasing, but I was as satisfied and happy as could be, and, was still involved in working with the parish youth. In fact, my young students liked me because I had turned the old church into a basketball court and kind of gymnasium.

Again, my time in this parish was short lived when the pastor of another parish (St Anthony's in National City) passed away, and the Bishop assigned me as pastor of the predominantly Hispanic parish. Ironically, before I even visited to introduce myself, a group from the parish called the bishop to request a younger priest, complaining that I was too old and knew very little Spanish. I certainly was up in age, but by this time I was speaking Spanish fluently, was eager to be challenged, and dared to be critiqued by people who had never even met me. The Auxiliary bishop, and of Hispanic heritage, called a parish meeting and corrected the misinformation. Well, what do you know? That was all I needed. I'll prove to them; how wrong they are! I thought. Ironically, when retirement came after two years, the parish that didn't want me petitioned the bishop to keep me as pastor of their Parish.

Chapter 28:
Retirement.

I pray for you the reader that you may discover the way to "BE ALL YOU CAN BE."

In December of 2003, I officially retired from active full-time ministry, but continued volunteering at other parishes. One day, while visiting the headquarters for the Sacred Fathers up in Wisconsin (the order to which I had previously been professed), I was introduced to a Franciscan priest (also visiting from San Diego). In our conversation he told me that he had just been transferred here to his Order's headquarters He mentioned that he had just left as chaplain to a new Catholic High. School in Del Mar and that the Principal was searching for a replacement. I immediately asked: Would you give me Name and phone number of that principal?" LO & BEHOLD! I had prayed that I might find a full-time job, and "voila!" Upon my return to San Diego, I immediately called the school principal, (Mike Deeley) a young man who loved his school, and without any interview or meeting I was hired for a job that I held for over sixteen years! Can you believe it? I half doubted I would find a full-time job, and there it was. Over sixteen years of ministry to more than 2000 students per year. This is where, once again, I encourage teenagers to "Be all you can be!"

It's been a long haul from the little town of Salina, Kansas, and moves or transfers to so many parts of the world. With challenging stops in Indiana, Asia, Europe, and Latin America Through it all I now see that word "passion" was the motivating secret to what I consider a rewarding life. And "BE ALL YOU CAN BE"? That's what athletes and famous people all over the world have been driven by. We all have to make a clear choice—drift aimlessly throughout your life and with absolutely no idea of how to take advantage of some hidden talent is sad situation. I often say to myself: "GOD DOESN'T MAKE JUNK!"

With memories of my ordination day and the years that followed still clear in my mind, I find it hard to believe that so much time has passed. I continue my service as a priest helping out at my retirement home here in San Diego. I never considered myself a talented individual, but I was always determined to never give up. my experiences. I hope, can inspire and convince young people to never give up on their dreams. Whatever the years ahead may bring, I remain committed to serving people of God and my Country.

BE ALL YOU CAN BE!

CIVILIAN SCHOOLING

1943: MINOR SEMINARY
1947: NOVITIATE ("Boot Camp") religious profession of three vows
1948-1956: POST GRADUATE STUDIES Hales Corners, WI
1956: ORDINATION TO THE PRIESTHOOD (MILWAUKEE, WI.)
1957: COMPLETION OF PRIESTLY STUDIES (GUADALAJARA, MEXICO)

MILITARY SCHOOLING

1966: US ARMY CHAPLAIN SCHOOL
1967...AIRBORNE SCHOOLS (BASIC & MASTER JUMP WINGS)
1967: SF "Q" (QUALIFICATION COURSE) ...OKINAWA
1976: CHAPLAINS ADVANCE COURSE
1979: COMMAND AND GENERAL STAFF COLLEGE
1987: ARMY WAR COLLEGE, CARLISLE BARRACKS, PA.
1983: LEADERSHIP EFFECTIVENESS: ATLANTA, GA.
1988: MID-MANAGEMENT; SAN DIEGO, CA.
1995; DEATH AND DYING: UNIVERSITY OF SAN DIEGO
1967; SCUBA AND HALO TRAINED

Acknowledgments

Fr. Pablo Sebastian de Soza, MC and Tina Chase were immensely helpful in writing this booklet. I could never have done this without their help.

Printed in the USA
CPSIA information can be obtained
at www.ICGtesting.com
LVHW010315280924
792310LV00017B/282